HELMSLEY & KIRKBY THROUGH THE AGES

THE STORY OF THESE ANCIENT YORKSHIRE MARKET TOWNS.

COMPILED AND WRITTEN
By
KEITH SNOWDEN

CASTLEDEN PUBLICATIONS,
PICKERING.

ISBN 0-9514657-4-0.

Also by Keith Snowden :
KINGS IN RYEDALE
PICKERING THROUGH THE AGES
THORNTON DALE THROUGH THE AGES
MALTON & NORTON THROUGH THE AGES.

Typeset, Printed and Bound
at the press of the Publisher :
CASTLEDEN PUBLICATIONS,
11, Castlegate, Pickering,
North Yorkshire, YO18 7AX, U.K.
Telephone (0751) 76227.

INTRODUCTION.

THERE is a thirst for knowledge of local history, both among indigenous and new residents. Also, those tracing their family trees—for genealogy seems to be a growing pastime — will find such a book useful for background material.

It may be as well here to remark on variations in the spelling of names, which depends on the recorder getting it right. In the case of my own surname, some people spell it erroneously as 'don'. From my own family records I know that there were Snowdens associated with Harome. Kirkbymoorside and Appleton-le-Moors. There are Snowdens connected with Spaunton and a family of Snowdons in the Helmsley area.

This book, which must be a short one, covers the parishes of Helmsley and Kirkbymoorside from the earliest times to the present day. There will be omissions, for it is impossible to record everything in so small a work, but there may, perhaps, be some surprises too.

K.S.
Pickering.
April, 1991

ACKNOWLEDGEMENTS.

THE AUTHOR wishes to thank the following for their help and co-operation during the researching of this book:
Arthur Brayshaw, John Buffoni, Nicholas Crookenden, Andrew Grayson, David Grayson, *Micro Metalsmiths*, Beatrice Pacitto, E. Winston Peel, Georgina Sellers and Isabel Warner.
    And for the loan of engraving of Helmsley (1799): John H. Rushton.

Photographs by the author.

TIMES LONG GONE.

HOW FAR back in time can one go to tell the story of a town and its surrounding area? When telling the story of Helmsley and Kirkbymoorside, one must go back further in time than the mind finds it easy to comprehend. At least there was animal life in the area in the Palæolithic period, or Old Stone Age, which has been placed at about three million years ago and until about 12000 B.C. This was the period which saw the emergence of primitive man. At that time tropical conditions existed and all kinds of wild animals, suited to such a climatic state, roamed the country. We have concrete evidence in this area through the discovery of the Kirkdale Cave, which has been described as: 'the most productive fossil bone cavern in Britain.' It was excavated by Professor William Buckland after it was accidentally found in 1821, and imbedded in the mud on the floor of the cavern were the bones of hyaena, lion, tiger, bear, wolf, fox, weasel, elephant rhinoceras, hippopotamus and three species of deer. It was concluded that the Kirkdale Cave was the home of hyaenas of the Pleistocene Period, which embraced in its latter part the Old Stone Age,

At that time it is believed that the waters of Lake Pickering had risen to the mouth of the cave and to have deposited a layer of alluvium which had covered the bones and preserved them.

As time rolled on there came a complete reversal in climate in which ice of enormous thickness formed over the whole of north-western Europe, According to the late Professor Percy F. Kendall this would have been around 25,000 years ago. The professor concluded that the great ice sheet of the North Sea had covered lower hills with glaciers, thus preventing drainage and streams and rivers, such as the Derwent, flowing into the vale were imprisoned, and thus Lake Pickering was formed. The overflow from the lake carved out deep gorges, such as the one at *Kirkham Abbey*. The Lake of Pickering stretched from Gilling in the west, to Sherburn in the east.

Following upon the Ice Age, as the waters gradually receded, marshlands and forests would develop, creating conditions suitable for the habitation of man in the Mesolithic era, or that period between the Old and New Stone Age. It is believed that men of that period visited the western part of our area, probably to hunt and fish, for traces of their summer camps have been found on the high ground above Helmsley. Neolithic man seems to have favoured the high ground and they progressed from savagery to a civilised style of life, learning how to make weapons from stone by grinding and polishing. Most importantly they developed agriculture and pottery-making. The Neolithic communities demonstrated an increasing strength of religious belief and careful burial of their dead.

The Bronze Age was brought in by the Celts about 1800 B.C., when Britain was invaded by the Gaels. Here was a civilisation much in advance of anything that had gone before. They used the alloy to manufacture weapons and tools, Their sepelchure mounds are scattered over the moors north of Helmsley. The Celts were followers of the Druid religion and believed in the immortality of the soul. Food, weapons and utensils were placed in the barrows for use by the dead. Helmsley is said to have been held sacred by the Druids, from whom a neighbouring valley has received its name of *Drudale Howl*, or *Druid's Dale*. Helmsley is said to have had many elm trees.

The Celts were Welsh-speaking people; the language of the Ancient Britons, and some of the names remain around Kirkbymoorside and Farndale, a striking example being the River Dove. We Yorkshire folk call our small streams becks, which is derived from *bechan,* and where it twists through a cleft in the hills, it is called a *gill*, examples being *West Gill Beck* and *Blakey Gill*. A stream that dries up in summer is called a *sych*, which

2

has become *syke*, examples being *Rawson Syke, White Syke, Sykes House,* and *Green Sykes.* A garden is a *garth* and at Helmsley there is *Canon's Garth Lane,* and at Kirkbymoorside *Tinley Garth.* Names beginning with *Pen* mean head, such as the head of a valley, or a hill, and there is an example in *Penry Holme,* on Skiplam Moor. *Forth* is a ford and there is a *Bowforth* near Wombleton. *Monket* would also seem to be a Celtic name derived from *Maen Coed,* meaning 'the standing stone in the wood.' *Ty* means a house in the Welsh language. There is *Lidsty Hill* near Lastingham.

The Bronze Age spanned approximately one thousand years and about 500 B.C. the Iron Age came in.

It took the Romans quite some time to subdue the north of England which was ruled by a warlike tribe called the Brigantes. The Roman's first serious conquest was in A.D.43, by order of the Emperor Claudius. The Brigantes were ruled by King Venutius who held out against the Romans. His queen was Cartimandua, to whom Caratacus, the son of Cunobelinus, the dead king of the Trinobantes, flew for protection when he lost his lands in western Britain after nine years of resistance. Instead of granting Caratacus refuge however, Cartimandua betrayed him to the Romans. The Brigantes had a camp at Malton and the Romans set up their fort on the site.

The main sphere of Roman interest seems to be in their roads from Malton to the coast, passing through Cawthorne Camps to Dunsley Bay, above Whitby. Small finds of Roman pottery have been made from north of Kirkbymoorside, near Gillamoor, Hutton-le-Hole and Appleton-le-Moors. Remains of Roman villas have been found at Hovingham and Beadlam Grange. Roman coins have turned up at Nawton, Skiplam, Appleton-le-Moors, Spaunton, Fadmoor, Douthwaite, Sleightholmedale and Lastingham.

Relics of Romano-British settlements have been discovered at Spaunton and Hutton-le-Hole. A bronze head

3

came to light at Gillamoor. The Romans brought Christianity to Britain, but when they withdrew their forces after A.D.400 to defend their own country, Christianity was driven back into Cornwall, Wales and Westmoreland by new invaders.

THE DARK AGES.

THE ANGLES, who originated around the mouth of the River Elbe, established themselves in East Anglia and Lincolnshire around 500 and conquering Yorkshire, settled around the Tweed. Ida established the Kingdom of Bernicia from the Tees to the Forth. Our part of Yorkshire became the Kingdom of Deira. Wales was never subjugated and when Romano-British institutions were swept away, England became a heathen country, Christianity surviving in Wales alone.

Kirkdale Minster is dedicated to St.Gregory, who, as Pope in 597 sent Augustine on a mission to Britain. The Venerable Bede tells an interesting story of Gregory and some slave children from Deira: I must here relate a story, handed down to us by the tradition of our forebears, which explains Gregory's deep desire for the salvation of our nation. We are told that one day some merchants who had recently arrived in Rome displayed their many wares in the Market-Place. Among the crowd who thronged to buy was Gregory, who saw among other merchandise some boys exposed for sale. These had fair complexions, fine-cut features, and beautiful hair. Looking at them with interest, he enquired from what country and what part of the world they came. 'They come from the island of Britain', he was told, 'where all the people have this appearance.' He then asked whether the islanders were Christians, or whether they were still ignorant heathens. 'They are pagans,' he was informed. 'Alas!' said Gregory with a heartfelt sigh, 'How sad that such bright-faced folk are still in the grasp of the Author of Darkness, and that such graceful features conceal minds void of God's grace! What is the name of this race?' 'They are called Angles.' he was told. 'That is appropriate,' he said, 'for they have angelic

4

faces, and it is right that they should become joint heirs with the angels in heaven. And what is the name of the province from which they have been brought?' 'Deira,' was the answer. 'Good, they shall indeed be rescued *De ira*—from wrath—and called to the mercy of Christ. And what is the name of their king?' 'Aelle,' he was told. 'Then,' said Gregory, making play on the name, 'it is right that their land should echo the praise of God our Creator in the word *Alleluia.*'

Bede also tells how King Aethelwald gave some land to Cedd, Bishop of the East Saxons, on which to build a monastery to which he himself might often come to pray and hear the word of God and where he might be buried. Cedd chose a site for the monastery among some high and remote hills, which seemed more suitable for the haunts of robbers and dens of wild beasts than for human habitation. When Cedd had been bishop of the province and administered the affairs of this monastery for many years through his representatives, he happened to visit the monastery during the time of a plague, and there fell sick and died. Many of the brothers died in that epidemic and with them King Aethelwald. This was in 659 and Bede tells us that Bishop Cedd [pronounced Kedd] was first buried in the open, but in the course of time a stone church was built, dedicated to the blessed Mother of God, and his body was reinterred in it on the right side of the alter.

Bede called this place *Laestingaeu* and it is generally accepted that Lastingham church stands on the site of Cedd's burial place. Certainly it is of great antiquity as a visit to the crypt will confirm. Of the ancient stones kept there is a dragon's head from the decorations on the Abbot's throne and it is said to be 8th century.

There is another school of thought, for when *St. Gregory's Minster*, at Kirkdale was rebuilt somewhere between the years 1056—65, a number of engraved stone coffin-lids were used to build the walls. One of them, which is now inside the church to prevent further deterioration, has been identified as that of King Aethelwald. Another,

5

also now inside the church, with an interlace design, and the tassels of a pall at the edges, was said to be that of Bishop Cedd, but others think it that of Orm, although that seems unlikely when we know that Orm was responsible for rebuilding the church. So, if Lastingham was *Laestingaeu,* what are those coffin-lids doing at Kirkdale?

For some reason King Aethelwald ceased to rule and became a monk. Perhaps he was weary of the power struggles which were a feature of those times.

Northumbria had promoted the Christian cause and it produced many great men of the church, such as Aidan, Wilfrid, Cuthbert and Chad. The latter had close connections with our area, for Bede tells us that Cedd bequeathed the Abbacy of the monastery of *Laestingaeu* to his brother Chad, who subsequently became Bishop of Mercia. In 665, King Oswy sent Chad to be consecrated Bishop of York, but on arriving in Kent, he found that Archbishop Deusdedit had died and that no successor had been appointed. He therefore went on to the province of the West Saxons and was consecrated as bishop. After the example of the Apostles, Chad travelled on foot and not on horseback when he went to preach the Gospel, whether in town or country, in cottages, villages or strongholds ; for he was one of Aidan's disciples and always sought to instruct his people by the same methods as Aidan and his own brother Cedd. It seems that Chad did not hold his bishopric for long as Bede relates that in 667 : The Mercians were at this time ruled by King Wulfhere, who on the death of Jaruman asked Theodore to provide him and his people with a bishop. Theodore, however, did not wish to consecrate a new bishop for them, but asked King Oswy to give them Chad as their bishop. Chad was then living quietly in his monastery at Laestingaeu, while Wilfrid ruled the Bishopric of York, and indeed all the lands of the Northumbrians and Picts to the borders of Oswy's realms......so Chad received the Bishopric of the Mercians and the people of Lindsey.

6

According to Bede, Chad still spent some time at *Laesti-ngaeu*, where in 672 he died and was buried close by *St. Mary's* church. In 1148, the relics of St. Chad were transferred to Lichfield, which had been the headquarters of his bishopric.

Bede was instructed in Latin and Divinity by Trumbert of Lastingham.

All Saints church, at Kirkbymoorside, is another example from the early days of Christianity. During the restoration of 1873, several Saxon crosses, covered with carved interlace work, were found embedded in the walls. In 1965, a silver coin was found by the sexton in the churchyard. It was a sceat, a coin of Ethelred, king of Northumbria, who was married to a daughter of the all-powerful King Offa. The coin was therefore late 8th century and may have been dropped in the churchyard during the days of the first church.

Another Saxon church was at Sinnington, on the same site as the present *All Saints* church.

During the 5th century, the names of many places ended with Anglian syllables, such as *-ton*, (Sinnington, Nawton, Appleton, Cropton, Hutton, Wombleton, Carlton, Spaunton, and Sproxton); and *-ley*, (Helmsley and Pockley); also *-ham*, (Lastingham and Hovingham). The *Boro' Beck*, at Helmsley, is said to have a Saxon name. The Anglo-Saxons preferred living in self-governing agricultural settlements, rather than towns.

THE NORSEMEN COME.

DUE TO poverty in the Scandinavian countries, the young men of that area took to piracy. They became masterly seamen and the animal figureheads on their long boats must have struck fear into many a breast. Their first attack was against Wessex in 790. Three years later they attacked Northumbria. *The Anglo-Saxon Chronicles* record: In this year dire forewarnings came over the land of the Northumbrians and miserably terrified the people;

7

these were terrible whirlwinds and lightnings, and fiery dragons were seen flying in the air. A great famine soon followed, and a little after that...........the ravaging of heathen men lamentably destroyed God's church at Lindisfarne with plunder and slaughter.

By 876 the invaders had overrun Yorkshire and Half-dan, the Dane, divided the lands of Deira among his followers. The monks were among the greater sufferers; the monasteries were plundered for their wealth. Lasting-ham and Kirkdale were destroyed. Our part of Yorkshire was totally subjugated, and whilst we have seen that many Celtic names have survived roundabout this particular area, Danish names now appeared, ending in -by, (Kirkby and Normanby) and -thwaite, (Douthwaite). Many Old Norse words remain in the North Yorkshire dialect.

Ulf was a sub-king of Deira and brother-in-law to King Canute. He owned vast tracts of land in the west of the region, some of which was at Wombleton, Nawton, Pockley and Edstone, and on becoming a Christian he gave large portions of his lands to *St. Peter's* church at York. It was the Danish custom when conveying property to hand over a drinking-horn. Ulf's Horn is one of the treasures of *York Minster*, which occupies the site of *St. Peter's* church. The church of *St. Michael*, at Great Edstone was given to *St. Peter's* by Ulf. The sundial at Great Edstone church informs us: LOTHAN WROUGHT ME. Poor Ulf was treacherously murdered on the orders of Canute in 1025.

It was somewhere after that time when *St. Gregory's Minster* at Kirkdale was rebuilt. The original church was destroyed during the Danish invasion. Simeon of Durham wrote of the Danish army: The army raided here and there and filled every place with bloodshed and sorrow. Far and wide it destroyed the churches and monasteries with fire and sword. When it departed from a place it left nothing standing but roofless walls. So great was the destruction that at the present day one can scarcely see anything left of these places.

8

Primeval cave : Kirkdale.

St. Gregory's Minster, Kirkdale.

The Market Cross, Helmsley.

The Boro' Beck, Helmsley.

The Anglo-Saxon sundial at Kirkdale is said to be one of the most complete in the world, and also bears the longest known inscription from Anglo-Saxon times. It is divided into the eight parts of the Saxon day. From the inscription we know that Orm, the son of Gamel, who must have been a local landowner, bought *St. Gregory's Minster* when it was in a ruinous state and rebuilt it from the ground in the days of Edward the Confessor and of Earl Tosti, or Tostig. According to a local legend it was intended to build the church nearer to Nawton and stone was taken to the chosen place, but during the night it was mysteriously placed at Kirkdale.

Siward, a great warrior, ruled Northumbria until his death in 1055. His son, Waltheof, was still a child so the kingdom was ruled by Tostig, who was the son of Earl Godwin of Wessex. Tostig was not a popular ruler and was often absent. While he was hunting in Wiltshire with the king, 200 thegns rebelled and slew all his household men and took all his weapons at York. In his place they chose Morkere, the brother of Earl Edwin of Mercia. Tostig went to Flanders for his safety. Tostig's brother, Harold, became king and Tostig was not to take that lying down, so he joined forces with Harald Hardrada, king of Norway, and a great battle took place at Stamford Bridge when Tostig and Hardrada were slain. The deployment of King Harold's army at York left the south undefended and the Norman invasion of 1066, by William the Conqueror took place.

NORMAN TIMES.

WILLIAM the Conqueror was the bastard son of the sixth duke of Normandy and he was 39 years old when he conquered the south of England. He was crowned on Christmas Day, 1066, by Aldred, Archbishop of York, in Westminster Abbey. He returned to Normandy and in his absence there were Saxon risings. The north of England was a particular sore spot and a general revolt took place in Northumbria, led by Waltheof in alliance with Sweyn, king of Denmark, Malcolm Canmore of Scotland and Edgar Atheling. The rebels captured York and slew the Norman garrison.

William returned and bribed Sweyn to withdraw his fleet from the Humber. As a lesson for their resistance, William carried out his terrible 'Harrying of the North'. In the open places and along the roads, the bodies of men were left to rot on the ground for there was none left to bury them; all had been cut off by the sword or through famine had fled their land. William spent the winter of 1069-70 laying waste to the country from York to the Tees. Leaving a few men to clear up the rebels, he headed south. His course led him through hills and valleys where the snow often lay while neighbouring districts were rejoicing in the bloom of spring. Through this wild region he now made his way amid the cold and ice of winter. It needed the bidding and example of a leader who was ever the foremost and who shrank from no toil which he laid upon others, to keep up the spirit of his followers. The march was toilsome and dangerous; the horses died in crowds; each man pressed on as he could, thinking only of his own safety and reckoning little of his lord or of his comrade. At one point William himself with six horsemen only, lost his way, and had to spend the night in utter ignorance of the whereabouts of his main army. But his fortune carried him through all dangers.

William arrived at Helmsley and from there made his way to York. There was a local saying that he swore to keep himself warm. 'Swearing like Billy Norman' was a phrase used in Bilsdale and the Cleveland Hills.

William took the land from the Saxon owners and gave it to many of his officers. In 1086 the great survey which we know as the *Domesday Book* was carried out. It is a useful record of our land at that time and for the first time many place names appear in writing. It also gives information on the previous owners of the land. Helmsley is referred to as *Elmslac* and at the time of the

12

survey it was held by three thegns, who had three-and-a-half carucates of land to be taxed and land for two ploughs. The largest manor was held by Ughtred and there was a wooden church with two priests. There were thirteen families. The name *Elmslac* is thought by some to have been derived from the many elm trees hereabouts. Another suggestion is that the place was named after a family called Helm. Yet another later spelling was *Hamlake*.

Kirkbymoorside was called *Chirchebi* and was held by Torbrant, who also held Hutton-le-Hole (*Hotun*) and Sinnington (*Sevenicon*). Kirkdale is also recorded as *Chirchebi* and was held by Gamel, who also owned Lastingham (*Lestingeham*), Spaunton (*Spantun*), Great Edstone (*Micheldestun*) and Little Edstone (*Parva Edestun*). Orm, the son of Gamel, had Gillamoor.

Sometime before 1122, the manor of Elmslac was given to William l' Espec, who founded the church of *St.Hilda* in Bilsdale. He was succeeded by his son, Walter l'Espec, who was a hardy warrior. According to the *Cottonian Manuscripts*, Walter had an only son, also named Walter, who was fond of riding his horse with exceeding swiftness. One day when galloping at a great pace his horse stumbled near a small stone, and young Walter was brought violently to the ground, breaking his neck and leaving his father without a heir. l' Espec gained consolation in the founding of three abbeys; at Kirkham, where the fatal accident is said to have happened; at Wardon, in Bedfordshire; and at Rievaulx. Abbot Aelred, of Rievaulx, has left us the following description of Walter: A man quick of wit, prudent in counsel, moderate in peace, circumspect in war, a true friend, a loyal subject. In appearance too he was remarkable — his stature passing tall, his beard long, his forehead wide, his eyes large and bright, his face broad but well-featured, his voice like the sound of a trumpet, setting off his natural eloquence of speech with a certain majesty of sound.

13

Rievaulx Abbey was the first Cistercian foundation in Yorkshire, and owed its existence to Walter l'Espec. *Burton's Monasticon* states: St. Bernard, abbot of Clareval, sent some monks to England about 1128, who were honourably received by both king and kingdom, and particularly by Walter l'Espec, who in 1131 allotted to them a solitary place in Blakemore near Hamelac, now Helmsley.

The monks at once proceeded with the erection of the monastery, which like all those of the Cistercians, was dedicated to the Blessed Virgin. The Abbey was amply endowed with landed property to the ammount of fifty carucates, of which nine were given by l'Espec, twelve by the Crown, twelve by Roger de Mowbray, and six by the bishops of Durham. There was also an extensive pasturage for upwards of 4,000 sheep and cattle in the neighbourhood, with free warren and other priveleges; but it is singular that not one donation of a church or chapel occurs, so that their spiritual income must have been very small.

The third abbot was Aelred, who was elected in 1160, having previously been abbot of Revesby, which was a colony or offshoot from the parent abbey of Rievaulx. Aelred, as a youth, had fled from the court of David, king of Scotland and afterwards wrote the life of that monarch. He was the author of many historical pieces, but is best known for his account of the Battle of the Standard. He died in 1166, and was buried at Rievaulx.

Archbishop Thurstan of York, during the contest between Maude and Stephen, chose Walter l'Espec as one of his leaders in the Battle of the Standard, which was fought in 1138. L' Espec was supported by Robert de Bruce, his son Adam, William de Albemarle, Roger de Mowbray, William de Percy and Bernard de Balliol. Hailes wrote: The aged and venerable Walter l' Espec ascended the carriage in which the Holy Standard was fixed, and harangued the surrounding multitude. He reminded them of the glory of their ancestors, and described the barbarities of the Scottish invaders.

14

'Your cause is just; it is for you all that you combat; I swear', said he, grasping the hand of the Earl of Albemarle, 'I swear that on this day I will overcome the Scots, or perish.' 'So swear we all', cried the barons assembled around him.

Our part of the country had suffered much from raids by the Scots, and the victory of the northern barons at Northallerton ensured peace for a while. L' Espec gave *All Saints* church, Helmsley to *Kirkham Priory*. He had *Canon's Garth* built to house the Augustinian canons of *Kirkham Priory*.

Later in life, Walter l'Espec retired to Rievaulx and joined the brothers. He died without further issue and was buried there.

At Kirkbymoorside, William the Conqueror evicted Torbrant, the Saxon owner, and gave the lordship to Robert de Estoville, or Stuteville, a Norman who had come over with the Conqueror. The family rose high in royal favour and figured largely in the annals of Norman England. It was this family who built the first castle at Kirkbymoorside on Vivers Hill. The Stutevilles were lords of Knaresborough and acquired much land to the north of York. In 1101, the barons, wishing to keep their estates and fearing the strong rule of King Henry I, he being an Englishman and married to an Englishwoman, rebelled and backed the claim to the throne of Robert, duke of Normandy. For his part on the side of Robert, who was defeated in 1106, Stuteville lost his lands, which were bestowed on Nigel de Albini, who married the heiress of the Mowbrays and assumed that name. It seems that the Mowbrays owned some land at Kirkbymoorside at the same time as the Stutevilles, but Robert de Mowbray had rebelled against William Rufus and was imprisoned for thirty years at Windsor. He died in 1106, and his vast estates, comprising 280 manors, devolved upon Nigel de Albini, Earl of Arundel.

At the Battle of the Standard, Robert de Stuteville fought alongside l'Espec, of Helmsley and was given

15

Kirkbymoorside as a reward by King Henry II, in 1156. William of Newburgh recorded that Robert de Stuteville was one the Yorkshire barons who minted their own coins. About 1190, Robert founded a priory for Benedictine nuns at Rosedale, and somewhere between 1183—99, William de Stuteville endowed a chapel at Gillamoor for a resident chantry chaplain to sing mass daily for the soul of the benefactor, and he also gave a house for the chaplain's use.

Following the death of Walter l'Espec, Helmsley manor was conveyed by the marriage of his youngest sister, Adeline, to Peter de Ros, or more correctly perhaps, Roos, as the family came from that place in Holderness. Robert de Ros, surnamed Furstan, built the castle at Helmsley, or Hamlake as it was then called.

The reign of King John was another stormy time for the northern barons, most of whom opposed John's misrule; prominent among them were Ros and Stuteville, both of whom refused to follow John abroad against France in 1213. The barons opposition caused King John to invade the north in 1216, when several castles were siezed and slighted. Helmsley is said to have been almost the only castle to withstand him. Robert de Ros was one of the Guardians of the *Magna Carta*. He died in 1227 and was buried at London.

There was a bridge over the Rye at Helmsley in 1250.

THE MIDDLE AGES.

IN THE Baron's War of 1263, William de Ros took the side of Simon de Montfort in his rebellion against King Henry III. Ros appears to have suffered no harm through this for by 1301, we are told, he was the wealthiest man in the Helmsley area and had two courtyards at his castle and manor.

William the Lion's grandson, King Alexander III, was accidentally killed while out riding when his horse stumbled and fell over a precipice. This caused a crisis in the

Scottish royalty, as all his children had predeceased him. There was a granddaughter, who had been born to Eric, king of Norway, and it was agreed that she should rule Scotland and be married to Prince Edward, the son of the English king. On arriving at Orkney, however, the 'Maid of Norway', as she was known, sickened and died, thus causing an interregnum. There were no less than thirteen candidates for the throne, including William de Ros. To avoid civil strife, the Scottish nobility asked King Edward to choose from the thirteen. Edward declared John Baliol to be the greater claimant.

Queen Isabella, the wife of King Edward II, usurped her husband in 1326. Ros joined Thomas, Earl of Lancaster, in assisting the queen. The king was cruelly murddered at Berkelely Castle, to the eternal disgrace of all those who were involved in that horrific deed.

Kirkbymoorside had connections with one of the most beautiful and romantic figures in English history. Joan, the daughter and heiress of Nicholas Stuteville, was called by Jean Froissart, the French chronicler, 'The Fair Maid of Kent'. When she was only twelve years old, she made a secret pact to marry Thomas Holland, who showed great prowess in the tournament-lists and became what in todays values would be a millionaire for his part in the capture of the Count of Eu at Caen in 1346. In that same year, the Scots invaded England and Joan is said to have been at Neville's Cross with Archbishop de la Zouche's army, when the Scots were defeated. This was also the same year the great plague, The Black Death, first came to Britain. It came from China, spread accross Europe following the trade routes and first appeared in the west country, then spread to the east. It was to visit another twice, by which time it had taken one-third (some say one-half) of the population. Richard Rolle, the hermit, who was born at Thornton Dale, recorded: Many churches were widowed of their clergy, but within a short time a great multitude of those whose wives had died flocked into Orders but of these many were illiterate and little more than laymen, except that they knew how to read, although they could not understand. As a result of the plague, Helmsleys population of 282 adults in 1377 had been mostly wiped out by 1353. Kirkbymoorside also suffered.

Joan of Kent was regarded as a heroine after the Battle of Neville's Cross, and shortly after she attended a ball at Calais where she accidentally dropped a garter. King Edward III picked it up and bound it round his knee, and immortalized it with the words: *Honi soit qui mal y pence*. [Evil to him who evil thinks]. Two months later, the king ordered twelve garters of royal blue, embroidered with the words he had uttered and the cross of St.George and gave these to the first knights of his Order. Thus was born one of the greatest orders of chivalry and a model for almost every order of European chivalry.

Joan did not dare reveal her secret contract with Thomas Holland and she was forced into a marriage with the Earl of Salisbury by her cousin the king. There was a great scandal and the earl had Joan thrown into prison. The great wealth of Holland was good enough for the Pope to annul the marriage and she was able to marry her hearts choice and through that gained the earldom of Kent. Thomas Holland died in 1360, leaving Joan with four children. She was by then thirty-two. The king's eldest son, 'The Black Prince', was still a bachelor and he shocked the king when, six months after Holland's death, he announced his bethrothal to Joan. They were married in St. George's Chapel, Windsor in the autumn. As they were cousins they had to have a papal dispensation to allow them to marry. Prince Edward died at the age of forty-five.

It was in 1349 that the Wake lands passed to the Countess of Kent, and so to Joan, the niece of Lord Wake. Joan resumed her maiden name and left the barony of Kirkbymoorside to her son Baldwin de Wake. The impression on her seal bore the device of a lady on a horse

Helmsley Castle.

All Saints' church, Kirkbymoorside.

High Hall, Kirkbymoorside.

Canon's Garth, Helmsley.

riding side-saddle, a style which she is said to have been the first to adopt. The Wake line ended in three co-heiresses, one of whom was married to Ralph Neville, Earl of Westmoreland. The Nevilles were one of the most powerful families in the north of England. Richard II conferred the title of Earl of Westmoreland upon Ralph Neville of Raby, who was said to have been a man of the greatest and most ancient of English nobility, as descended from Ucthred, Earl of Northumberland. Earl Ralph, by his wife Joan, daughter of John O'Gaunt, Duke of Lancaster, had so great an issue, and the name of Neville became so greatly multiplied that almost at the same time there flourished, besides the Earl of Westmoreland, and Earl of Salisbury, and Earl of Warwick, an Earl of Kent, a Marquis Montacute, a Duke of Bedford, a Lord Latimer and a Lord Abergavenny—all Nevilles.

The War of the Roses, fought from 1455—71, found the Yorkshire nobles divided. On the Duke of York's side were the Scropes of Bolton and Masham; most of the Nevilles, headed by the Duke of York's brother-in-law, Richard Neville, Earl of Salisbury, who in 1452—3 had engaged in a private war with the Percies of Northumberland; Lord Fauconberg of Newburgh, George, Lord Latimer of Danby, Snape and Well; Lord Lumley and John Mowbray. Among the Lancastrians were the families of Percy, Clifford, Ros, Mauley, Dacre, Talbot, Greystoke, and Stafford, and the Tudor earls of Richmond. Lord Thomas Ros, (not to be confused with the Scottish Lord Ross) took part in the Battle of Hexham in 1464. Lord Montague trapped the Lancastrians on the banks of Devil's Water. Ros and Hungerford were caught

21

hiding in the woods and along with Sir Thomas Fynderne and six others were beheaded at Newcastle-upon-Tyne on the 28th of May.

In 1482, Helmsley Castle passed to Richard, Duke of Gloucester (later King Richard III) bv his marriage with Ann Neville, the daughter of Warwick 'The Kingmaker'.

Ralph Neville, the second earl of Westmoreland, who was an invalid, died in 1484. During the period 1465— 76, George Neville was Archbishop of York.

At Kirkbymoorside the Nevilles built a new castle at the northern extremity of the town. Most houses at that time would be made of wood, based on the cruck, or 'A' construction and plastered with wattle and daub. The roof would be covered with thatch. *High Hall*, in Castlegate, Kirkbymoorside, is said to have originated in 1492.

TUDOR TIMES.

FOLLOWING UPON the death of King Richard III, in 1485, and after passing through seventeen generations of Ros's, Helmsley was conveyed in marriage to Sir Robert Manners, of Ethall Castle, Northumberland. His grandson, Thomas, to whom the Ros titles and lands descended, was advanced to the dignity of Earl of Rutland in 1525.

Ralph Neville, third Earl of Westmoreland, died of grief at the loss of his only son in 1523.

The reign of King Henry VIII heralded a long period of religious strife which was to run through several reigns. In January 1536, the two agents Legh and Layton arrived in York to begin their survey of Yorkshire monasteries and nunneries, which was the prelude to the suppression of the religious houses. They appear to have travelled haphazardly, but fairly swiftly. One may question the validitity of their report when reading:

Item. to Yedingham, nuns of St. Benedict order, of the foundation of Lord Latimer three miles from the aforesaid place.

Item. to Keldholme, nuns of the Cistercian order, of the foundation of Lord Westmoreland ten miles from the aforesaid place. Legh wrote: All the cuntre makythe exclamacions of this abbot of Riwax. [Rievaulx].

The gentry were staking their claims for pieces of the carve-up to come. The Earl of Westmoreland 'beseeches Cromwell to have him in mind for Blanchland and Keldholme.' In the meantime King Henry started the process of getting rid of his queen, Anne Boleyn, On April 24th a special commission was appointed to try a number of men who had been associating with the queen. Among the special commissioners was the Earl of Westmoreland. The result was that five men were charged with having illicit intercourse with the queen, one of them being her brother, Lord Rochfort. The Earl of Westmoreland was also on the jury at the trial of the queen and her brother, when they were sentenced to death. Thomas, Earl of Rutland was also a member of the jury.

Before the carve-up of the religious houses came the 'Pilgrimage of Grace', and many of the landed gentry got swept along with it, the pressure coming from the people, many of whom were related to the priests and nuns of the religious houses. If the gentry tried to hold themselves aloof, they were threatened with death. The rising began in Lincolnshire in October 1536, but it soon spread into Yorkshire, led by Robert Aske, a lawyer. Couriers brought news to Aske at York that the commons of Durham were hasting to join him, bringing with them Lord Latimer, (the husband of Katherine Parr and owner of Sinnington) the Earl of Westmoreland and Lord Lumley. Lord Latimer was a reluctant participant, as we can see from a letter he wrote in January 1537, while returning from London: —that the commons of Richmondshire, grieved at my coming up to London, have entered my house at Snape and will desroy it if I come not home shortly. If I do not please them I know not what they will do with my body and goods, wife and children.

Lord Latimer and the Earl of Westmoreland were lucky

23

to escape any serious consequences for their part in the 'Pilgrimage of Grace'. The king was not entirely convinced that Lord Latimer was forced into his stance, for he had been advising Aske. Both the nobles, were Nevilles, however and after all, the king was related to them through his mother.

The suppression of the monasteries went ahead. How it was done depended on the abbot; if he cooperated with the king's agents, money would be saved, but he would expect something in return for a peaceful surrender. In 1538, Rievaulx was surrendered by Richard de Blyton, who received a pension of £66-13s-4d; and twentythree monks received £99 divided amongst them. The gross income of the monastery at that time was £315-14s-6d, and the net, £278-10s-2d per annum. The plate of the church, 516 ounces in weight; 100 fodders of lead and five bells, were surrendered into the hands of the commissioners.

After the dissolution came the distribution of the monastic lands. Thomas, Earl of Rutland, was granted the site of *Rievaulx Abbey* in exchange for other lands. Anthony Belasyse was given *Newburgh Priory*. The site of *Rosedale Abbey* was granted to the Earl of Westmoreland, together with the manor of Keldholme, to be held by military service. *Byland Abbey* was surrendered in 1540 by John Ledes (or Alanbrig), the last abbot, and twentyfour monks. Their gross yearly revenue was £295-5s-4d, and there were 516 ounces of plate. This with the seven bells in the church, the furniture and lead stripped off the roof ammounted to 100 fodders, were sold for the king's use.

The poor are always with us, and there were plenty of poor people at Kirkbymoorside, for Charles Neville, the sixth Earl of Westmoreland: took common lands from the tenants and enclosed them, which was the only relief of the inhabitants of the town, wherein they kept every man one, two or three kine for the relief of themselves, their wives and children.

A cottage industry was spinning, carried out by the female members of the family on the spinning wheels. In this way linen was manufactured from yarn.

Yarn is an income, and the huswives thread
The larder fills with meat, the bin with bread.

It was in 1568 that Queen Elizabeth had Mary Queen of Scots imprisoned.

The unlucky Mary was moved about a lot during the months leading up to her death; and there is a tradition that she spent a night at *Arden Hall*, a former nunnery, near Hawnby. Mary was a Roman Catholic, and so were the Nevilles. Charles Neville convened a meeting of the northern nobles, which became known as 'The Rising of the North'. The Dukes of Northumberland and Norfolk gave their support, as well as Thomas Markenfield and Richard Norton. Norton had been one of the leaders of the 'Pilgrimage of Grace' and had held important posts, such as Sheriff of Yorkshire, member of the Council of the North, and governor of Norham Castle. Others taking part were Lumley, Plumpston, Tempest, Oglethorpe, Swinburne, Danby of Beeston, and Neville of Liversedge. There was a traitor in the camp, however, in the person of the Earl of Westmoreland's cousin, Robert Constable of Flamborough, who acted as one of William Cecil's spies, and who: 'proposed to trap them that trust me as Judas trapped Christ.' Norfolk and Lumley were arrested in the autumn of 1569. Both Northumberland and Westmoreland were summoned to court, but refused to go. Instead they gathered together a company of 500 horse and on Sunday November 14th as twilight was darkening entered Durham and strode into the cathedral, with 60 followers armed to the teeth behind them. Norton, with a massive gold crucifix hanging from his neck and carrying the old banner of The Pilgrimage of Grace, the cross and streamers and the Five Wounds. They overthrew the communion board, tore the English Bible and Prayer Book to pieces replaced the ancient altar, and caused mass to be sung with all solemnity.

Whilst they gained much support, they were doomed to failure. Charles Neville, sixth Earl of Westmoreland, had a blacksmith in Kirkbymoorside make him some 're-versed' horseshoes and by this means eluded his pursuers in deep snow and made his escape into Scotland. As late as 1823 the descendants of the smith enjoyed a house in Castlegate, Kirkbymoorside at a rent of one farthing a year. Charles died in exile in 1601 and all his lands were confiscated by the Crown. The castle at Kirkbymoorside now declined and the *High Hall* grew in importance. According to tradition there was a secret passage from the cellars of the hall to a cottage in Crown Square, which had a priesthole.

William Camden published *Britannia,* a Latin survey of Great Britain in 1586, in which he mentioned the Boro' Beck at Helmsley and remarked of it that the water disappeared at about a mile below the town, and rose again at *Harum,* a few miles below.

Helmsley Castle was improved for residential purposes in the middle of the 16th century on the orders of Edward Manners, the Earl of Rutland and Lord of Helmsley, 1563—87. *Canon's Garth* was rebuilt in stone and much of that work still remains.

26

A family related to the Nevilles were the Brookes, who purchased monastic lands during the reign of Henry VIII. One was a Lord Mayor of York and his wife, Lady Brooke died in 1600 and an interesting brass to her memory is in the church at Kirkbymoorside. It reads as follows:

> Prepare for death for if the fatal sheares
> Could have been stayd by prayers, sighes or tears
> They had been stayd, and this tomb thou seest here
> Had not erected beene yet many a yeare.

Here lyeth the body of my Lady Brooke, who while she lyved was a good woman, a very good mother, and an exceeding good wife. Her soul is at rest with God, for she was sure her Redeemer lived, and that though worms destroyed her body, yet shee should see God in her flesh. She died the 12th of July 1600.

The brass has a portrait of Lady Brooke kneeling with her eleven children.

JACOBEAN TIMES.

LADY Catherine Manners, the only daughter of the sixth Earl of Rutland, was married to George Villiers, first Duke of Buckingham, in 1620. Villiers was a favourite of King James I, of whom Sir John Oglander wrote: The King loved young men, his favourites, better than women, loving them beyond the love of men to women. I never yet saw any fond husband make so much or so great a dalliance over his beautiful spouse as I have seen King James over his favourites, especially Buckingham. The King is not well without him, his company is his solace. The king declared to his Council in 1617: I, James, am neither a god nor an angel, but a man like any other. Therefore I act like a man and confess to loving those dear to me more than other men. You may be sure I love the Earl of Buckingham more than anyone else, and more than you who are here assembled. I wish to speak on my own behalf and not to have it thought to be a defect, for Jesus Christ did the same and therefore I cannot be blamed. Christ had his John, and I have my George.

27

Buckingham received great riches and power and Helmsley passed into his ownership. He is said to have begged Kirkbymoorside of the king as a garden.

Much rebuilding took place in 1633 at *St. Gregory's Minster*, Kirkdale, when a low-pitched roof was erected. Alterations were made to Kirkbymoorsides old inn, *The Black Swan*, when the wooden portico was added in 1632 by William Wood. There were a number of unlicensed ale houses in the town and beer was brewed at the *Rectory* by Robert Otterburn, A *Grammar School* was built in Job Hall Street, [now Church Street] and although it has been altered and modernised, it is still in use as a library.

During the reign of Charles I, the Bishop of Durham had to flee from his See as there was a Scottish invasion. The bishop took refuge in Helmsley Castle. The Scots got as far south as Ripon, but were bribed to return home.

In 1644, during the Civil War, Helmsley Castle was held for the king by Colonel Crossland. It was besieged by Sir Thomas Fairfax who commanded the Parliamentary forces. A party of royalists from the garrisons of Skipton and Knaresborough attempted to relieve the besieged, but they were repulsed by Fairfax's soldiers. Colonel Crossland made a long and brave defence, but in the end he had to capitulate. He was allowed to march out with his colours, but one of the articles of surrender specified : that the castle of Helmsley be absolutely demolished, and that no garrison hereafter be kept there by either party. During the process of dismantling, one side of the keep was blown to pieces by a terrific explosion and nearly everything else was destroyed.

George Fox, the celebrated Quaker, visited Malton and Pickering in 1652. A Quaker Meeting was established at Kirkbymoorside at the time by Roger Hebden, a woolen draper. The way of the Friends was not an easy one and in 1654 Roger Hebden was writing from York Castle, where he was incarcerated, to George Fox : Great is the

28

work in the dales above Kirbymoorside. In 1655 and 1656, John Brookbank and George Robinson of Farndale each had a Bible taken from their homes for refusing to pay money demanded by the priest at Kirkbymoorside, for repairs to the church.

With the coming of the Commonwealth in 1653, Helmsley Castle went to Sir Thomas Fairfax. Oliver Cromwell died five years later and was given a State funeral and was buried in *Westminster Abbey*. Cromwell's son, 'Tumbledown Dick', was not strong enough to maintain the Commonwealth and King Charles II was restored to the throne in 1660. Cromwell's body and those of his supporters, Henry Ireton and John Bradshaw, were exhumed and dragged through London on open hurdles to Tyburn. They were first hanged and then taken down and beheaded and their fingers and toes hacked off also. Their heads were later stuck up on *Westminster Hall*. There are two or three stories as to the final resting-place of Cromwell's body; the most likely being that Mary, Countess Fauconberg, Oliver's daughter, had it brought to *Newburgh Priory*. There is a sealed chamber in the house which is thought to be where the body is concealed.

Mary, the daughter of Lord Thomas Fairfax, married George Villiers, second Duke of Buckingham in 1657, after his return from abroad. Villiers had been a favourite of King Charles II, but he was hated by others and ridiculed:

Stiff in opinion, always in the wrong,
Was everything by starts and nothing long;
But in the course of one revolving moon
Was chemist, fiddler, statesman, and buffoon.

Deprived of wealth he retired to Helmsley and made some repairs to the castle. His income from rents was said to be £50,000 per annum, but that he squandered it in dissipation and became an outcast of society. He made a racecourse at Helmsley, for he loved riding and hunting.

In 1687, Villiers was out fox-hunting near *Bumper Castle Farm*. Whilst waiting for a fox to be dug out, he took a chill and was carried to Kirkbymoorside and put to bed in the house of one of his tenants; not as Alexander Pope, who was no lover of Buckingham, put it:

> *In the worst inn's worst room, with mat half-hung,*
> *The floors of plaster, and the walls of dung,*
> *On once a flock-bed, but repaired with straw,*
> *With tape-tied curtains, never meant to draw,*
> *The George and Garter dangling from that bed*
> *Where tawdry yellow strove with dirty red,*
> *Great Villiers lies—alas! how changed from him*
> *That life of pleasure, and that soul of whim!*
> *Gallant and gay in Cliveden's proud alcove,*
> *The bower of wanton Shrewsbury and love;*
> *Or just as gay at council, in a ring*
> *Of mimic statesmen, and their merry king.*
> *No wit to flatter left of all his store!*
> *No fool to laugh at, which he valued more.*
> *There, victor of his health, of fortune, friends,*
> *And fame, this lord of useless thousands ends.*

It was in the house next to the inn, now called *Buckingham House*, where, on his deathbed, he uttered: 'The world and I shake hands, for I daresay we are heartily weary of each other. Oh! what a prodigal have I been of that most valuable of all possessions, Time!' The parish register recorded his death so: 1687. April 17th, George Vilaus, lord dooke of bookingam.

The old bridge at Helmsley was rebuilt in 1667.

Religious troubles had continued for 130 years. the problem being what to do about Roman Catholics and Dissenters. During the reign of King William III a law was passed allowing moderate Dissenters to open churches of their own and worship as they desired. Extreme Dissenters, such as Quakers; although the laws still allowed them to be imprisoned, William often allowed their release after a short term. Called The Toleration Act of 1689, it

Old Grammar School, Kirkbymoorside.

Rectory House, Helmsley.

Buckingham House, Kirkbymoorside.

Stately home: *Duncombe Park.*

caused many Friends to register their homes for Quaker worship. Houses at Helmsley, Bilsdale, Kirkbymoorside, Fadmoor, Welburn, *Hutton i' the Hole,* Farndale and Rosedale were registered. John Snowden at Harome, Will Proud at Wrelton, George Pearson of Rosedale, Will Hick of Kirkbymoorside, George Sowerby and Will Stockton in Farndale, all registered their homes at later dates.

High Hall, in Castlegate, Kirkbymoorside became the squire's home and was occupied by the Hobson family.

Puritanism had grown since the Reformation and protestant zealots railed against some of the old country customs which probably pre-dated Christianity. A local chronicler recorded: In the year 1708 there did come a great company of Broad Brims for to stop the May Dance about the pole at Sinnington, and others acting by concert did the like at Helmsley, Kirby Moorside and Slingsby, singing and praying they gat them round about the garland pole whilst yet the May Queen was not yet come but when those with flute and drum and dancers came near to crown the Queen the Broad Brims did pray and sing psalms and would not give way while at the finish up there was like for to be a sad end to the day but some of the Sinnington Bucks did join hands in a long chain and thus swept them clean from the pole. At Slingsby there was a great dordum of a fight, but for a great while the Broad Brims have set their faces against all manner of our enjoyment.

GEORGIAN DAYS.
Helmsley, once proud Buckingham's delight,
Slides to a scrivenor, or a city knight.

CHARLES DUNCOMBE was a member of Parliament and Lord Mayor of London in 1708. In 1695 he bought the Helmsley and Kirkdale estates from the trustees of the Duke of Buckingham and in 1718 he erected *Duncombe Park* from the designs of Sir John Vanburgh and built by William Wakefield in the Doric style and the front of the house was considered to be of great architectural skill and combination. The hall was a magnificent room some sixty feet long and forty wide, surrounded by fourteen lofty Corinthian pillars and was ornamented with a number of busts of Greek and Latin poets, with large medallions of the twelve Cæsars. The saloon was eightyeight feet by twentyfour and formed into three divisions by Ionic pillars and was elegantly adorned with antique statues and family pictures.

Charles Duncombe died unmarried in 1711, leaving his property to his sister Ursula, the wife of Thomas Brown, who assumed the name of Duncombe.

Kirby Mills, long associated with milling through the *Keldholme Priory*, had new mills built in 1719. This was an age for building and at Kirkbymoorside many fine houses were built in stone. Some of the earlier wood and plaster dwellings were reconstucted in stone. The old castle of the Nevilles would make a convenient quarry.

Up to that time each town and village had land that was worked in the traditional method with each householder having his strip. We have noted earlier how the common holders of Kirkbymoorside were robbed of land by the Neville lord of the day. Now came acts of Parliament which allowed the very wealthy to gain more land; the Inclosure Acts —a form of legalised robbery in which the rich got richer and the poor got poorer. Sharp off the mark was Charles Duncombe, who had several daughters and wanted to increase his income to pay for their marriage dowries. Duncombe got the ownership of the whole 300 acres at Fadmoor in 1763. The three freeholders were left with 86 acres between them and 117 acres were left for common grazing.

A later Act dragged on for a number of years. It was originally instituted in November 1781 by Charles Slingsby Duncombe. Objections were later raised by the vicar of Kirkbymoorside, who was probably acting for other freeholders. Negotiations for the sale of rights began in January 1789. The Society of Friends in Kirkbymoorside had proved their claim for the 'two ancient messuages now used as a meeting house', and a minute records that they had sold their two 'rights' for £30. Many such sales were made during the next few months, the owners selling out rather than having to meet the costs on the very small area that was allocated to one house. Joseph Shephard of Douthwaite bought out 40 people. George Simpson of Sleightholmedale bought out 17 claims. Duncombe got 1,389 acres; the vicar, William Comber, 49, and the rest shared 662 acres between them, making a total of 2,100 acres enclosed.

In the Award document the occupations of most of the proprietors are given: 46 yeomen [small farmers], 5 weavers, 1 flaxdresser, 2 tallow chandlers, and one each of the following: cooper, butter factor, common brewer, and peruke [wig] maker.

The old bridge at Helmsley was washed away by a severe flood in 1754 and was rebuilt.

Oliver Goldsmith wrote *The Vicar of Wakefield* in 1766 and it has been thought that Kirkbymoorside may possibly have been in his mind when he described the series of catastrophes that befell the unfortunate clergyman in his novel.

The churchyard gates at Kirkbymoorside, leading from Crown Square, are dated 1767.

Lord Feversham's daughter, Anne Duncombe, married Robert Shafto of *Whitworth Hall*, County Durham. He had previously been engaged to a daughter of Sir Henry Belasyse of Brancepeth, Her unrequited love caused her to die of a broken heart. Her story inspired Peacock to write a song, based on the old Northumbrian bagpipe tune *Brave Willy Foster*, now better known as:

> *Bobby Shafto's gone to sea,*
> *Silver buckles on his knee;*
> *He'll come back and marry me,*
> *Bonnie Bobby Shafto.*

A portrait by Joshua Reynolds reveals him as a handsome

yellow-haired man of fashion. He was Member of Parliament for Durham from 1760—68, and afterwards he represented the borough of Downtown, Wiltshire. He was a shipowner and only occasionally went to sea. He died in 1797 and was survived by his wife, Anne, who lived to the age of 101, dying in 1872.

The following letter appeared in *The Yorkshire Magazine* of 1786:

June 27. This day, as some workmen were digging for limestone in a quarry near a mile to the N.E. of Kirby-moorside, they discovered a great number of human bones in a cleft in the rock, several yards from the surface of the ground. The incident having excited my curiosity, I went to the place yesterday, and found the bones much broken by the populace; on searching among them I discovered a mutilated under jaw of a hog, and part of the bone of a sheep's leg, which was more found than any of the others, owing I suppose to the desenses of its parts. I was told there was bones of horses, &c among them; but as I did not see any others but what appeared to be human, cannot say whether there are or no. I was also informed that when they were first taken out of the rock there were nine skulls, and 18 scapulæ, or shoulder bones, the fragments of which are dispersed everywhere among the rest, but could not find one entire, their thinness and porosity having made them less able to resist the air than the others. I found part of a tibia, or shin bone of a child, which from its structure, seems to have been ricketted.

I do not hear that anybody can yet give an account why they have been deposited in such an uncommon place, either from history or tradition; perhaps the most probable conjecture may be, that this has been the receptacle of the slain in some battle that may have been fought on the common, in a very steep part of which the rock is situated; and, what makes it more likely, the chasm seems to have been open at the top at some time, though now closed by some natural cause, as the position of the stones indicate by their lying not horizontally, but rather arch-wise over the top. A small distance upon the plain is a hill, which from its form and situation, may perhaps contain more of those relics.

Some of your more learned correspondents may probably be induced to look into the histories of ancient times and thereby throw more light on the matter.

I am, &c. W.Bearcroft.

This William Bearcroft, who resided in Castlegate, Kirkbymoorside, was born at Pockley in 1763 and died in 1830. There is a brass to his memory in the Parish church which pays tribute to his 36 years instruction of youth *aided by industry and perseverance is sufficient under Divine Providence to form the man of science; himself untaught furnished an example.*

During the 1700s The Society of Friends, to give the Quakers their correct name, were active in the area. There was a burial ground at Lowna. John Richardson of Hutton-le-Hole was a most prominent member and he travelled extensively, not only in Britain, but in the American colonies. William Stockton and John Snowdon were appointed Overseers at Kirkbymoorside. There were a number of women 'ministers' at Kirkby: Anne Richardson of Hutton, also Ann Snowdon, Rebecca Turner, Elizabeth Hunter, Bridget Fletcher, Dorothy Stockton and Mary Snowdon. Men recorded as ministers were: Samuel Skelton of Wrelton, Christopher Stockton, Leonard Snowdon and William Stockton. A journal of the life of John Richardson was published in 1757 and it was selected for the library of Ackworth School, when that famous Quaker academy was established in 1779.

John Wesley, the founding Methodist, visited Helmsley in April 1764.

Mrs. Shephard of Douthwaite had a share in at least one whaling ship that sailed out of Whitby. It may have been that she had a share in Captain William Scoresby's ship, *The Henrietta*. Scoresby was born at *Nutholme*, Cropton in 1760. He became one of the great whaling skippers and made a fortune for the shareholders of *The Henrietta*.

37

John Jackson, the son of a tailor, was born at Lastingham in 1778. In 1804 he exhibited at the Royal Academy and eventually received the full honours of that artistic institution. He made a copy of Correggio's *Christ in the Garden of Gethsemane,* with figures increased to life size, for Lastingham church, when he paid for restoration work in 1828. The picture is still in the church, although not in its original position.

The Georgian days were a curious mixture; on the one hand many fine buildings were constructed, which would seem to indicate wealth. On the other hand, the Industrial Revolution had started and to country areas it meant poverty. In the past men had harnassed the forces of nature to provide power for the fulling and corn mills, but by the end of the 18th century the steam engine was replacing traditional power. When the 19th century came in the writing was on the wall for the cottage spinners as production was switched to the large towns on a greater scale. The people in the Helmsley and Kirkbymoorside area had to rely mainly on agriculture to scrape a living. Many tradesmen had to combine two or more businesses to eak out a living.

It was also the beginning of an age of church and chapel building—a religious revival. In 1800, the Wesleyan Methodists erected their chapel in Bondgate, Helmsley. At Kirkbymoorside the tower of *All Saint's* was rebuilt in 1802.

William Wordsworth, the Lake District poet, wed his childhood playmate, Mary Hutchinson, who was residing with her brother at *Gallows Hill,* Brompton-by-Sawdon, on October 4th, 1802. They spent the night at *The Old Manor House,* Helmsley and visited Rievaulx the following day. It was night when they reached Sutton Bank and It is claimed that the Hambleton Hills inspired William to write his sonnet, *Dark and more dark the shades of evening fell.* In that same year, *St.Aidan's* church at Gillamoor was rebuilt, almost single-handedly, by Joseph Smith.

Helmsley claimed a 'Methuselah' in Thomas Martin who died at the age of 130 in 1804.

When Admiral Horatio Nelson was killed at Trafalgar in 1805, Commodore Wrightson, of Kirby Mills, was present at the scene of death.

The Independent Church had a chapel in Tinley Garth, Kirkbymoorside, as early as 1793. The minister from 1813—26 was the Rev. W. Eastermead who wrote a history of Kirkbymoorside and district.

A directory of 1823 informs us that Thomas Pape, postmaster, in Castlegate, Helmsley, received letters from York at five in the morning and despatched letters at two in the afternoon. This was a horse post, a system which had been operating in more populous areas since 1680. The postboy was usually a youth riding a single horse, with a portmanteau behind him for the letters. He was expected to keep up a pace of seven miles per hour in summer and five in winter. There were four carriers to run errands and collect or deliver goods to and from the neighbouring markets : William Simpson made journeys to York on Mondays and Thursdays, staying overnight. William Wood set off to Thirsk at three o'clock on Monday mornings and returned the same day ; and to Kirkbymoorside on Tuesdays at one in the afternoon. John Pearson came from Scarborough to *The Black Swan*, arriving at seven of a Friday evening and returning to Scarborough at two the following afternoon.

There were two academies, one for boarders and another for day pupils. The Rev. George Simpson's was in the Market Place and John Wood's *National School* was in Church Street.

Four blacksmiths had the Christian name of John ; Clark senior and Clark junior were both in the Market Place. Cooper was in Castlegate. John Mason combined his smithy with a hardware store, in Bondgate. There were five butchers and five boot and shoe makers. Richard Myers had a drug store in the Market Place. Thomas

39

and John Barker were bacon and butter factors. L. Snowden's shop was in Church Street. W.W.Bentley was in the Market Place, as was Simeon Hutchinson, who was also agent for The Norwich Union Fire Insurance Company.

Six inns were listed: *The Black Swan*, where licensee Matthew Agar was also the excise officer. *The Board* [now *The Feversham Arms*], *The Crown; The Golden Lion*, which was in the Market Place; *The New Inn*, a posting house, in Boroughgate; and Ann Pape's *Royal Oak* was in the Market Place. Sarah Sigsworth was a maltster and spirit dealer. There were three surgeons: Robert Harris, Job Ness, and John Sandwith, all in the Market Place. Five tailors were listed: Charles and James Betts, both in Pottergate; Thomas Cooper in Bondgate; Robert Johnson in Castlegate; and John Webster in Church Street.

Candles made of tallow fat were widely used for lighting, but were not as pleasant-smelling as wax candles. John Cowen, Charles Shout, and William Smith were tallow chandlers. Thomas and Richard Warrener were wheelwrights, the former in Bondgate, the latter in Pottergate. Thomas Barrick and William Ward were saddlers. John Fenwick was the corn miller, and George Ward the gunsmith.

80 pupils received free tuition at a charity school through the support of Charles Duncombe.

Helmsley was listed as *Helmsley upon The Black Moor;* whereas Kirkbymoorside was listed as *Kirkby*, or *Kirby-Moor Side,* where Robert Cooper, of Crown Square,was the postmaster; the horse post arriving from York and Helmsley at 8 a.m. and departing at 12 noon. Among the townspeople catalogued were William Bearcoft; and Lavinia Garbutt, Hanah Harrison, and Hanah Petch (Gentlewomen). Thomas Harrison was the coroner. John Watson's academy was in Jobs Hall Street [now Church Street]. William Ellerker, in the same street, was a gardener. Chris Ellerker was the ropemaker in Piercy End.

The Black Swan, Kirkbymoorside.

The Crown, Helmsley.

Helmsley Town Hall.

All Saints' church, Helmsley.

There were three attornies: Thomas Boyes, William Garbutt and Robert Petch. George Potter was the bacon and butter factor. The three blacksmiths were Thomas Carter, of Piercy End; William Garbutt, of Market Place; and John Pilmer, of West End. No less than ten boot and shoe makers kept the people of Kirkby shod, including James Dobson; Matthew Ellerker; William Hebron: James, Robert, and John Sample. The six butchers included John Blakeclock; George Bower; and Robert Hornsey.

William Lockey was the druggist, in the Market Place. George Potter and Thomas Gibson were flax dressers, of which there were five. Robert Sunley and Brook Judson were coopers. The eight grocers and tea dealers included George Potter, Joseph Ainsley, Thomas Dawson, William Hugill, William Wood, Jeremiah Warrener, and Messrs Cole and Frank.

Of the ten inns and taverns listed, seven were in the Market Place: *The Black Swan*, where John Potter was also brewer and maltster; *The Dog & Duck* of Richard Ransome; William Wood's *George & Dragon*: John Atkinson's *Green Dragon*; John Leng's *Hare Inn;* Henry King's *King's Head* and William Smith's *Queen's Head.* Peter Snowden's *Crown* was in Crown Square, as was William Chapman's *Red Lion. The White Horse* was recorded as a posting house, in West End.

Kirkbymoorside had a printer, Robert Cooper, in Crown Square, and a bookbinder, A. Jefferson, of the Market Place. Thomas Reed was the excise man. John Robinson had the corn mills at How End and at Kirby Mills. George Wake was a machine maker. There were three straw hat manufacturers, (which shows the popularity of that headwear): Hanah Baines, Jane Clark, and Elizabeth Kay. The three surgeons were Richard Chapman, Thomas Harrison, and Joseph Shepherd. Joseph Conning, George Hall, John Hardy, and John Jackson were all tailors. Five carriers served the town: George Pearson ran to Malton on Tuesdays and Saturdays, departing in the morning at five and returning at six in the evening. John Pearson came to *The White Horse* from Scarborough, arriving on Fridays at three in the afternoon, and leaving Saturday evenings at six. John Wood, from Pickering, came at three on a Friday afternoon and returned at six in the evening. Joseph Worthy ran to Malton on Tuesdays and Saturdays at five in the morning, returning at six in the evening. John Wrightson gave a service to York on Thursdays, returning the following day. He also gave an occasional service to Malton.

It is interesting to note that many of the family names mentioned in the directory are still known to this day.

In 1821, the Rye Bridge at Helmsley was widened. It was that same year when some quarrymen accidentally discovered the Kirkdale Cave, which was excavated in the same year by Dr. William Buckland, the Dean of Westminster, who wrote about it, reading a paper before the Royal Society in 1822. The cave extended in a zigzag direction about 300 feet into the rock, although it was later blocked beyond the first 20 feet. Bones from the cave were taken to museums all over Britain. The opening was quite small, being less than 5 feet square and the cave varied from 2 to 7 feet in breadth and height.

Charles Duncombe was created Baron Feversham in 1826. He married Charlotte, the only daughter of the second Earl of Dartmouth, and they had seven sons and three daughters.

A spate of church restoration and rebuilding began in 1827, when *St.Gregory's Minster* had a stone tower added to replace a wooden belfrey. The church of *St.Lawrence,* at Rosedale was rebuilt by subscription in 1839, at a cost of £665. *All Saints'* church, at Helmsley, was drastically rebuilt in 1849, and from 1861—68. The restorations were started by the first Earl of Feversham and were completed by the second earl.

We have seen that the rich got richer and the poor got poorer, and that the people were forced to work on the

44

land. In 1795, the Whig Government began making allowances to unemployed, or low paid workers. As a result, employers (in many cases farmers) tended to pay low wages and employ labour on a casual basis. The cost of Poor Relief from 1813 to 1834 was above £7 million a year. Whole parishes were living on this form of dole. The result was that a new Act was introduced in 1834, by which no able-bodied person could obtain relief except by entering a Poor Law Institution — the dreaded Workhouse! A 'Poor House' was built at Kirkbymoorside in 1850, at a cost of £1,350; in the low side of Tinley Garth. Helmsley Poor Law Union covered no less than 72,885 acres. There was a Workhouse in Pottergate, but a new one was built in High Street in 1851.

John Sandwith, the surgeon at Helmsley, died in 1825. Colonel Bentham Sandwith of the Bombay Light Cavalry died at Cannes in 1850; and Lieutenant-General William Sandwith, C.O.B. of The East India Company, died at Helmsley in 1855.

THE VICTORIAN AGE.

BY 1840 there was a coach running from *The Black Swan*, Helmsley on Mondays, Wednesdays and Fridays to York at 9 a.m., and to Kirkbymoorside at 6 p.m. From *The Black Swan*, Kirkbymoorside, one ran to York on Mondays, Wednesdays and Saturdays.

Wesleyan Methodism continued to flourish and the chapel at Helmsley was enlarged in 1852. At the same time, a Wesleyan Day School was erected in Bondgate. A small Roman Catholic church, dedicated to St. Mary, was built in 1867, on the road to Rievaulx. There was opposition from the vicar of Helmsley, the Rev. Charles Norris Gray, M.A. A highly respected churchman, he was the son of Robert, Bishop of Capetown, to whose memory Vicar Gray built the chapel of St. Aelred in Helmsley church in 1821. There is a crucifix in the chapel which Rev. Gray brought from Oberammergau, where he had been to see the Passion Play. Vicar Gray maintained that there had been a church at Helmsley since 200 A.D., and he had a fanciful frescoe painted depicting St. Aidan preaching and King Oswald translating to the Angles of Hamlake. Other wall paintings in the church and some stained glass windows were executed under his direction, after the restoration of 1868. Vicar Gray took a keen interest in the welfare of the workhouse residents. He was instrumental in getting the uniform of the children in the institution banned, so that they could wear ordinary clothes, indistinguishable from other children. He had a paramour installed in *Rectory House,* his own residence being in Bondgate.

William, the second Baron Feversham, who had married Lady Louisa Stewart, the daughter of the Earl of Galloway, died in 1867. He was succeeded by his eldest surviving son, William Ernest, who, the following year was created Viscount Helmsley and Earl of Feversham.

At Kirkbymoorside the old Tollbooth was destroyed by fire in 1871 and rebuilt. The stone is supposed to have come from the castles.

The Railway Age had arrived and the country went railway crazy, people investing in all sorts of companies. Pickering had a horse-drawn railway service to Whitby as early as 1836, but it was not until George Hudson, the Railway King, bought the company and modernised it with steam locomotives in 1846 that expansion took place. On October 9th, 1871 the Gilling to Helmsley branch line was opened with a station at Nunnington. Gilling had been linked to Thirsk and Malton in 1853. Helmsley was linked to Kirkbymoorside on January 1st, 1874, and in April 1875 the line was opened from Kirkbymoorside to Pickering. The smoothness of the ride was attributed to the workmanship of Messrs Stead of Appleton Wiske and Kirkbymoorside.

Thus these towns were now joined by rail to the whole of Britain. One line that never got off the ground was a light railway linking Sinnington with Lastingham and Rosedale. One of the promoters was Horatio Bottomley, who founded *The Financial Times* and other famous publications. He got too involved in forming companies and eventually served seven years penal servitude. The Railway Age had its effect on the towns and Piercy End, at Kirkbymoorside, was renamed Railway Street.

Duncombe Park house was completely destroyed by fire on January 11th, 1879 and some of the valuable art works also perished. The house was rebuilt to the original plans in 1893. The south wing suffered a further fire in 1895, but it was rebuilt with the addition of a chapel.

Further rebuilding took place at *St. Gregory's Minster*, Kirkdale, in 1881 when the chancel was reconstructed by the University of Oxford.

The first General Election after the passing of the Franchise Extension and Redistribution Bill took place in 1885. Mr. E.W.Denison contested the seat for the Conservaties and Mr. Arthur Pease stood for the Liberal cause. Denison won with a majority of 340. The entire area came under the Whitby Parliamentary Division. During his term of office, Mr.Denison assumed the name of Beckett. He stood again the following year against Colonel Clayhill of Whitby, who was a Gladstone Liberal. Beckett's majority reached its zenith with 1,138 votes. In the 1892 election Beckett had a majority of 1,083 over Frank Pyman, a member of the Whitby shipowning family, who stood for the Liberal cause. Never again would there be such a large majority for the Conservatives in the remaining days of the Whitby Division.

The church of *St. Nicholas* at Bransdale was rebuilt in 1886 to replace the old chapel of *St. Mary*, believed to have been built about 1690.

The population of Helmsley in 1821 was 1,520. By 1881 it had reached the figure of 2,377. Kirkbymoorside had

2,181 inhabitants at the 1881 census. Helmsley in 1890 had a printer, William Allenby, who was also the chemist and had *The Ryedale Cocoa House.* James Allenby had had a printing shop as early as 1840. There was also a coachbuilder named Thomas Barker. H. Magson was a marine stores dealer. Richard Raper was the veterinary surgeon. George Rivis had *The Ryedale Roller Flour Mills.* Mary Sturdy was the ironmonger and Robert Sturdy the tinner, plumber and glazier, in Church Street. John Edwin and Christopher Sunley were painters and decorators. Joseph Snowden, of Bondgate, was both butcher and farmer. There were five academies and schools, with seperate *National Schools* for boys and girls. There were four blacksmiths and seven boot and shoe makers, or dealers. Only four hotels were listed: *The Black Swan, The Crown*, a posting house; *The Feversham Arms,* formerly *The Board Inn;* and *The Royal Oak.* Hugh William and Robert Pearson were solicitors, as was also Robert junior. J.R.Reid and F.W.Dowker were in partnership as surgeons while Dr. J.F.Porter practiced individually.

Mails from York arrived at 6.40 a.m. and letters were despatched at 9.40 a.m. and 6 p.m.

At Kirkbymoorside the printer was William Hardy in Church Street. He was also secretary to the Kirkbymoorside Gas & Water Co. Ltd., at Piercy End. Another printing concern was Lumley & Sons, at Dale End, who were also chemists, dentists, stationers and photographers. Another chemist was George Peacock, who was also a wine merchant and chemical manure manufacturer. The former *Grammar School* was now the *Reading Room.* John Sonley, in West End, was a baker noted for his traditional Christmas gingerbread, the wooden moulds for which are now in the *Ryedale Folk Museum* at Hutton-le-Hole. John Sonley & Son were coopers. Included among the six blacksmiths were Joseph Dowson, in Railway Street; and George Russell, of West End. Both these are names long associated with wrought iron work and agricultural machinery and engineering. There were seven boot and shoe makers and eight dealers. C.Conning was both butcher and cattle dealer. Joseph Conning was a grocer.

There were eight hotels, inns and taverns : *The George & Dragon*, *The Black Swan*, *The Cricketer's Arms*, *The Crown*, where Wilson Conning combined inn keeping with flour, ham and bacon factoring : *The King's Head*, *The The Red Lion*, *The White Horse*, a posting house ; and *The White Swan*.

George Porrit, James Sample, and Robert Sonley were listed among the six joiners. There were three refreshment rooms. Robert Petch was a local solicitor, a member of a family which had long been associated with the legal profession. The Dawsons were a well-known local family ; Edward was a plumber, another Edward was a musician, and George was a tailor. There were seperate *Board Schools* for boys and girls, and Miss Emily Waind had her academy in West End, whilst the Misses Annie and Emily Waterhouse were at *Ryedale House*.

An old Christmas custom at Kirkbymoorside was the ringing of the 'Frumity Bell' at six o'clock. Frumity was made by soaking pearl wheat and flavouring it with treacle and spices. It had to be eaten in silence, no one leaving the table until it was finished.

On December 4th, 1893 was born one of Kirkbymoorside's most famous sons. Sir Herbert Read, the son of a farmer at *Muscoates Grange*, who died when Herbert was ten. Herbert and his brothers were sent to *Crossley's School* at Halifax. At fifteen he left school and went to work in a bank, but he attended evening classes. An uncle lent him money so that he was able to go to Leeds University where he was intended to study law, but became more interested in literature and artistic subjects. During the first World War he served as an officer in the Green Howards, earning the M.C. and D.S.O. Some of his finest poetry is in his war poems. Following Samuel Taylor Coleridge's advice that an author should seek regular employment,he became in turn, a civil servant, assistant keeper at the *Victoria & Albert Museum*, a lecturer at Trinity College, Cambridge, then at Edinburgh University, editor of the *Burlington Magazine* and a partner in a publishing company. He was a professor at Harvard, U.S.A. and made lecture tours of Italy, Austria, Switzerland, Greece and America. In 1949 he moved to Stonegrave and bought the *Old Rectory*. As a literary critic and philosopher, Sir Herbert has been compared to John Ruskin. He had books published throughout his life from 1915. He died at Malton on June 12th, 1968.

THE TWENTIETH CENTURY.
THE RYEDALE LAUNDRY at Kirkbymoorside was founded in 1900 by a Miss Kendall and her partner to provide work for women in the area. Later the business was taken over by a Mr. Markham and after him it passed to Messrs T.Leadley and F.Moss.

King Edward VII came to Helmsley in 1901 to lay the foundation stone for the new *Town Hall*, which was designed by the famous architect, Mr. Temple Moore as a market hall and courthouse to replace the old tollbooth.

In the General Elections of 1895 and 1900 Mr.E.W.Beckett had been unopposed. In 1901, on the death of his uncle, Lord Grimthorpe, he was raised to the peerage and succeeded to the title. This caused a by election and Gervase Beckett, the brother of the late member, stood for the Conservatives. The result was a sensational victory for the Liberal candidate, Noel Buxton, with a majority of 445 votes. Many a Liberal's child was named after Mr.Buxton, although Beckett won the seat the following year by 71 votes. Gervase Beckett was to hold the seat until 1918 when the Whitby Division was abolished and the Thirsk and Malton constituency was created.

Joseph Sleightholme. of Kirkbymoorside, was a veteran of the Crimean War. He died at Kirkby in 1908. Born there in 1831, he enlisted in the 3rd Battalion Grenadier Guards at the age of twentytwo. He spent sixteen months in the trenches at Sebastapol and earned the Crimean and Turkish medals.

Coronation celebrations for King George V began at 6 a.m. in Kirkbymoorside on June 22, 1911, when the band assembled on the church tower to play the National Anthem. The jubilations culminated with a bonfire on Vivers Hill at 10 p.m.

The Rev. Charles N. Gray, vicar of Helmsley, died in 1913, having been incumbent since 1870. He was laid in state, and the schoolchildren were filed past his open coffin. He was buried with great pomp and ceremony when Cosmo Gordon Lang, the Archbishop of York, headed a large entourage of clergymen, in a church filled to overflowing.

The 'War to end all wars' broke out in 1914 and proved to be a terrible waste of young lives. One of Helmsley's casualties was Lieutenant Alwyne Morton Francis Worsley Porter of the 1st Battalion Lancashire Fusiliers, who was killed at the age of twentyfour while leading his men in an assault at Gallipoli.

William Ernest Duncombe, first Earl and third Baron Feversham, died in January 1915 at the age of eightysix. Archbishop Lang officiated at the funeral ceremony. The earl was succeeded by his grandson, Charles William, who in 1916 formed the Yeoman Rifles, a battalion of the King's Royal Rifles. He married Lady Marjorie Greville of Warwick, an illegitimate daughter of King Edward VII, a monarch well-known for his profligacy. Earl Feversham was killed on the battlefront in 1916. The third Earl, Charles William Slingsby Duncombe, was only in his tenth year when he succeeded to the barony.

The death of the second earl put crippling death duties onto the estate, but a solution was found in 1925, when

51

Duncombe Park became a boarding school for young ladies. It was later named *The Queen Mary School*. The family moved to *Nawton Towers*. Lady Marjorie married Sir Gervase Beckett, the ex-M.P.

It was in 1925 that Alan M. Moss took over the Ryedale Laundry from his father. As a boy he had helped with deliveries on the horse-drawn van.

A world-famous business started in 1927, when Frederick Slingsby, a Scarborough cabinet maker, at the instigation of Major Shaw opened a factory at Kirkbymoorside to manufacture gliders. *Slingsby Sailplanes* were leaders in the field and the *Kirby Kite* earned a universal reputation. German pilots, after the first World War, were not allowed to fly powered aircraft; consequently many were trained in gliders. Leading officers of the *Luftwaffe* were visitors to the Kirkbymoorside factory.

John Petch, the last practising member of an old legal family long connected with Kirkbymoorside, died in 1929 at the age of seventyseven. A brass in *All Saints'* church commemorates his passing.

Charles William Slingsby Duncombe, third Earl Feversham, married Lady Ann Wood, daughter of Edward, Lord Halifax, on May 9th, 1936, in *York Minster*. It was in that year that Duncombe was made Parliamentary Secretary to the Ministry of Agriculture. He was Lord-in-Waiting from 1934 until 1936.

During the second World War the 22nd Dragoons were encamped in *Duncombe Park* grounds. The park was well-wooded in those days and army vehicles were hidden underneath the trees to screen them from the air. Among the soldiers stationed there was Ian Carmichael, later to become a famous light comedy actor who appeared in many films. In 1944, the Earl of Feversham was promoted to Lieutenant-Colonel in the 13-18th Royal Hussars.

William Houlston died on October 25th, 1946. He had been a churchwarden for fifty years. A seat in the porch

Market Day at Kirkbymoorside.

Old Mill, Keldholme.

of Helmsley Parish church commemorates his service.

A disastrous fire destroyed the *Ryedale Laundry* premises at Kirkbymoorside in 1948, but the laundry was rebuilt the following year.

The Conservative government of 1951 was unsympathetic to railways and employed the infamous Dr. Beeching to axe the branch lines. On Saturday January 31st, 1953 the last passenger train from Pickering to Kirkbymoorside departed on a very stormy day. Rather ominously a chimney was blown off the Sinnington Station house and crashed through the glass top of the platform. The Railway Age for Helmsley and Kirkbymoorside had come and gone in less than a century. Piercy End got back its original name, which came from the Percehays, a medieval family who lived there.

George Buffoni, a former printer with the *Daily Express*, served in the army and was demobbed at *Duncombe Park*. As his papers printing works had been bombed out, he had no job to go back to, so in 1954 he took over the old Allenby printing shop at Helmsley and created the *Ryedale Printing Works Ltd*. Mr. Buffoni was later joined by his son, John, and the business expanded.

It was to Ryedale that a royal duke came to find his bride and to bring to York all the glitter of a royal wedding for the first time in over six hundred years. It was through his mother, Princess Marina's friendship with some Ryedale residents that the Queen's cousin, the Duke of Kent, came to meet his Yorkshire bride. Miss Katherine Worsley was a mutual friend of a family at Keldholme and the Duke was stationed with his regiment at Catterick. Much of the courtship was spent in Ryedale and included visits to the cinema at Pickering.

On June 8th, 1961 the Duke of Kent married Miss Worsley, of the Ryedale village of Hovingham in *York Minster. The Yorkshire Gazette* described it as a 'White Rose Wedding'. Queen Elizabeth II and her consort, Prince Philip, the Duke of Edinburgh; Princess Margaret and her husband, Mr. Anthony Armstrong-Jones; the Queen Mother and Earl Mountbatten headed the list of distinguished guests. After the reception at *Hovingham Hall*, the Queen flew back to London to attend an operatic performance.

Charles William Slingsby Duncombe died in 1963 and with him went the earldom, for he had no son, although the barony continues. Charles Anthony Peter Duncombe, a distant relative of the late earl, inherited the barony at the age of eighteen.

Christopher Shaw was born in Yorkshire, but graduated from the Massachusetts Institute of Technology with a Bachelor's degree in Mathematics and a Masters in Metallurgy. After working in America, he returned to his native Yorkshire and founded *Micro Metalsmiths* at Kirkbymoorside in 1964. As jobs in agriculture declined, due to the increased use of machinery, a light industrial factory was a welcome addition to the economy of the area. Workers from Pickering also found work at Kirkbymoorside. The *Slingsby Sailplanes* company had expanded and were manufacturing pre-made joinery, which created even more jobs. Unfortunately, shortly after the company changed hands, a catastrophic fire destroyed the premises in 1968. The new company was taken over by the well-known engineering firm of Vickers.

A sports complex, which included an open-air swimming pool, was opened at Helmsley in 1969, as a memorial to the late Earl of Feversham. The opening ceremony was performed by the late Duke of Norfolk.

In the 1970s a house-building boom started and this attracted a great number of new residents to Kirkbymoorside. Unfortunately, this has led to some competition between industrial expansion and residential development Some industrialists feel that the policy of the Ryedale District Council favours private housing development and some companies have had to seek space elsewhere. This is not a very happy situation for young people in the area, for as I write, unemployment is rising.

Lord Feversham wished to return to his ancestral home, *Duncombe Park*, and in order to raise money to achieve his aim and make the house open to the public, he sold off some of his estate cottages in Helmsley, some of which have been converted into shops which cater for the tourist. Where Kirkbymoorside had become residential, Helmsley has become a tourist mecca. In 1985, the girls school lease ran out affording Lord Feversham the opportunity to forward his plans and during the following five years he used local craftsmen to equip the house and it was opened to the public in the Spring of 1990.

John Buffoni moved his *Ryedale Printing Works* to Kirkbymoorside in 1987, occupying part of the site which had for many years been used for Russell's agricultural engineering works. Mr.Buffoni took the opportunity to further expand his business by installing the latest equipment which included an Akiyama four-colour printing press. Since then he has added another Akiyama and employs 48 full-time workers, printing full colour brochures and also on synthetic materials. They also print Bingo tickets.

Traffic and tourism are having a great impact on the two towns as we approach the end of the century. Kirkbymoorside has been able to boast that it has not had double yellow lines in its streets, but as this book goes to the press, they are on the way. Market days continue to attract crowds, but the cattle markets are long gone.